Module 4: Essay Writing

Introduction

In higher education, it is necessary to be able to structure and organise essays in an appropriate way, according to academic conventions. This module provides an introduction to academic essay writing. It guides you through the process of structuring an essay so that you are prepared for the kind of writing you will have to do in a typical UK academic institution. You will have the opportunity to develop your ideas and to produce detailed essay outlines on topics such as traffic congestion, English as a global language and urban overcrowding. By the end of the module, you will be better able to interpret essay questions and understand what lecturers expect from you. You will be able to tackle the process of writing an essay in a more organised and systematic way, moving from a clear plan and outline to a well-organised and well-written essay with an effective introduction and conclusion.

Contents

W0010071

1 Getting organised

At the end of this unit, you will be able to:

- understand the requirements of writing an academic essay
- analyse essay questions
- organise ideas to produce a clear outline

Task 1 What is an academic essay?

There are several different types of academic essay. For example, you might have to write:

- a descriptive essay
- an argument essay
- a comparison essay
- a cause and effect essay
- a problem–solution essay

Some essays may be a mixture of different approaches and types, but you need to be clear what sort of essay you are writing.

1.1 Match the essay titles (a–e) with the essay types above. Note that sometimes you will need to combine categories.

a. What are the main arguments for and against the implementation of very high rates of taxation?

argument

b. Road transport is inexpensive, convenient and one of the most flexible modes of transport, but it is not as eco-friendly as other methods. Discuss.

_____

c. Trace the history and development of environmentalism from the 1950s to the end of the 20th century, using examples of environmental issues to illustrate your answer.

_____

d. Discuss the problems faced by international students in the UK. Suggest and evaluate possible solutions to these problems.

_____

e. The increase in online shopping is only one factor in the decline of the British high street. Discuss.

_____

1.2 Whatever the essay type, the structure of an essay is generally similar. The purpose is to help the reader understand what the writer wants to say.

Write down what you think form the three main parts of an academic essay.

a. _____

b. _____

c. _____

1.3 Work with a partner or in small groups to discuss the aspects of an essay. Make notes of your discussion and present your conclusions to the class.

The introduction:	What is it for?
	What makes a good introduction?
The essay structure:	What is a paragraph?
	How do you show where a paragraph begins and ends?
	How do you decide the order of paragraphs?
The conclusion:	What is it for?
	What makes a good conclusion?

1.4 The purpose of this module is to improve your essay-writing skills. As a starting point, evaluate your current skills in specific areas.

Score your competence in the eight areas (a–h). Use a scale of 1 to 5 (1 = poor, 5 = excellent). Compare your answers with a partner's.

a.   writing correct and accurate English

b.   planning an outline of an essay

c.   drafting and redrafting my writing

d.   editing and proofreading

e.   organising information

f.   organising my time

g.   finding and using source material

h.   paraphrasing other people's words

Task 2 Analysing the essay question

2.1 The instruction verbs in the box are commonly used in essay questions. Think about their meaning. Then discuss your ideas with a partner.

> analyse   describe   comment   compare   discuss   evaluate   exemplify   identify

2.2 Read the essay question. Find and underline the key ideas it asks you to write about.

> Discuss the problems associated with traffic congestion. Suggest possible solutions and evaluate their effectiveness.

2.3 What *exactly* does the essay question want you to do? Circle the instruction verbs in the question. Then think carefully about the kind of essay you need to write. Discuss your conclusions with the class.

2.4 Ask yourself questions related to the three key elements of the essay question. Begin with *Discuss the problems associated with traffic congestion.* **Think about the three questions below. Then add one more question.**

   a.   What exactly is traffic congestion?

   b.   Where would you find traffic congestion?

   c.   What are the main causes of traffic congestion?

   • _____

2.5 **Work with a partner to discuss the rest of the essay question** *Suggest possible solutions and evaluate their effectiveness,* **using the same procedure in Task 2.4.**

   _____

   _____

   _____

   _____

2.6 Work in small groups to discuss your questions and answers. Present your conclusions to the class.

2.7 Work in small groups to discuss possible solutions to any aspect of traffic congestion. Choose three possible solutions and write them on a piece of paper. Exchange your solutions with another group and evaluate the effectiveness of the other group's solutions.

Task 3 Brainstorming ideas

Brainstorming involves free association, or rapidly generating ideas on a topic. Try these two different ways of brainstorming.

Free writing

This is where you quickly write down every idea you have that could be relevant to the topic. You can write a list or draw a mind map. The aim is to produce lots of ideas, so the form is not important. You do not need to worry about correct spelling or grammar – it is the ideas that are important.

Group brainstorming

This is where all the members of a group contribute their own ideas on the topic, 'bouncing' their ideas off each other.

3.1 **Use free writing to brainstorm the following topic:** *Transporting goods by road.* **You have two minutes.**

3.2 **Now complete a group brainstorming activity.**

a. Start individually. Think about the following topic: *Banning lorries from towns and cities.* Accept any ideas that come into your head.

b. Work in groups. Appoint a chairperson to write down your ideas. Then brainstorm the topic.

Task 4 Organising your ideas

Now that you have a set of ideas, they need putting together in an organised way. One method is to use a mind map to try to represent your ideas in a visual form. This can be very useful when you want to quickly see the relationship between your main topic, main ideas and supporting ideas. You write the main topic in the middle of the page and place the main ideas around it, connected with lines or arrows. Similarly, you write the supporting ideas around the main ideas, connected with lines or arrows.

4.1 **Look again at the essay question in Task 2.2. Below is a skeleton mind map of the essay topic you are developing. Complete the mind map with your ideas for solutions so far.**

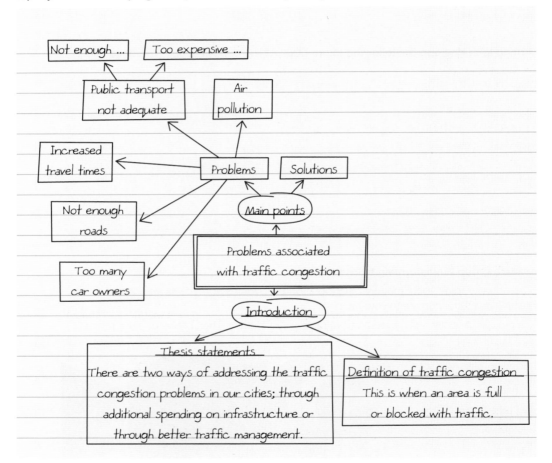

4.2 **Using your mind maps, work in groups to discuss the possible content of your essay, the introduction and main points.**

Reflect

Analyse the essay question below and brainstorm ideas for its content. Alternatively, do this for an essay question you are required to complete.

Discuss the problems associated with urban overcrowding and evaluate possible solutions.

At the end of this unit, you will be able to:

- start writing an essay
- write a thesis statement
- write an effective introduction

Task 1 What to include

Once you have begun to organise your ideas in a logical way, you need to decide:
- how to structure your essay
- how (and where) to include these ideas

In other words, you need to make decisions about the main sections of your essay.

1.1 **You might want to include the ideas (a–f) in your essay on traffic congestion. Think about the importance of each idea. Label them important (I), useful (U) or not important (NI). Work with a partner to discuss any other items or topics you can think of.**

a. A definition of traffic congestion. `I`

b. An explanation of the causes of traffic congestion. ☐

c. Your views on traffic congestion. ☐

d. A list of solutions to the problem. ☐

e. Examples of traffic problems in your hometown. ☐

f. Arguments in favour of or against possible solutions. ☐

1.2 **Decide the order in which the ideas should appear in the essay. Which idea will you need to spend most time on? Compare your answers with a partner's.**

Task 2 Information gathering

In academic writing, it is not enough to use your own ideas without any supporting evidence. It is essential to include relevant information from academic sources to give them 'academic weight'. You should obtain this information by thoroughly researching the topic, using a variety of sources. Make clear notes of any information you find. You can then use this information, with references, to support your argument. (See the *Referencing & Avoiding Plagiarism* module in the TASK series.) Keep a record of all your sources, when you collect the information, as it is easier to do this at the time, rather than later.

2.1 **Work with a partner to discuss possible academic sources. Write what you think will be your four main sources of information.**

a. _____

b. _____

c. _____

d. _____

2.2 **Number the points in the order of difficulty for you. Then discuss your answers with the class.**

____ finding appropriate sources

____ paraphrasing in your own words

____ understanding how much use to make of external sources

____ referencing in an appropriate way

2

Task 3 Arousing interest: The introduction

The *introduction* acts as a window to the rest of your writing. A good introduction should make your reader want to read your work. You can encourage interest by using a variety of different techniques.

For example, you can use one or more of these techniques:

1. a surprising or interesting fact
2. a question
3. a quotation
4. a definition
5. some important background information

3.1 **Which of the techniques (1–5) has the author used in the introduction to an essay entitled** *The education system in your country***?**

> The education system in your country
>
> According to a recent survey, a significant proportion of the population in my country has serious literacy problems.

3.2 **Read the essay titles (a–d). Write a sentence to use as an introduction to each one, using one of the techniques (1–5). Try to interest the reader so as to encourage him/her to read the rest of the essay.**

a.
> Family structure in your country.

_____

_____

b.
> The criminal justice system in your country.

_____

_____

c.
> Imports and exports to and from your country.

_____

_____

d.
> Transportation in your country.

_____

_____

Task 4 Writing a thesis statement

An introduction should also contain information on how you will develop the topic in the essay title. You write this in the *thesis statement*. This is a statement of your standpoint or the view taken in the essay. It should be concise and convincing. Your thesis statement is the controlling idea of your essay that you will develop in the main body.

You normally follow the thesis statement with a clear indication of how you will structure the main body of your essay in support of your thesis statement.

4.1 Identify the controlling ideas of the three thesis statements below. How do you think the rest of the essay will be developed in each case? What areas will be covered?

> Example
>
> Thesis statement: *The rise of English to global status is related to three main factors – economic, political and historical.*
>
> This essay will discuss the reasons WHY English has become a global language, with a specific focus on the ECONOMIC, POLITICAL and HISTORICAL reasons.

a. *The criminal justice system in my country functions in a variety of ways.*

b. *Although the Big Bang Theory is widely accepted, it will probably never be proved, and it, therefore, leaves a number of difficult and unanswered questions.*

c. *The key to coping with the rise in sea levels is education on its effects and the accurate forecasting of its hazards.*

4.2 Continue each thesis statement with a sentence outlining the structure of the essay, beginning: 'This essay will ...'.

4.3 Look again at the ideas you brainstormed in Unit 1 on traffic congestion. What is your own view about possible solutions to the problems? Identify your main idea and write it as the controlling idea in a single sentence. This will be your thesis statement.

4.4 What will you focus on? How will you develop your thesis in the main body of your essay? Write a follow-on sentence beginning: 'This essay will ...'.

2

Task 5 An effective introduction

An introduction should generally move from the general to the specific.

5.1 The sentences (a–e) are an introduction to an essay about the problems associated with urban overcrowding. Put the sentences in the correct order (1–5).

a. ___ As a result of this migration, modern-day cities face a number of serious problems related to overcrowding. ☐

b. ___ People were, therefore, drawn towards living in towns and cities for simple economic reasons. ☐

c. ___ This essay will identify solutions to these problems of urban overcrowding and evaluate their feasibility. ☐

d. ___ The most critical problems include homelessness, inadequate health care and education, unemployment, and knock-on effects such as rising crime and drug abuse. ☐

e. _1_ The 20ᵗʰ century saw a major increase in the world's population and, at the same time, the emergence of a society driven by the forces of economics and industry. G

5.2 Look again at the sentences in Task 5.1. Work with a partner to answer the questions.

a. Mark the general statements with a 'G'. How do they attempt to interest the reader?

_____

b. Mark the thesis statement with a tick. What is the controlling idea? How do you expect the rest of the essay to be organised?

_____

c. What are the minimum number of paragraphs you would expect in this essay? What can you predict about their content?

_____

5.3 The questions below can act as a checklist when writing an introduction. Read the checklist and think about how helpful this will be for you.

Introduction checklist

- Is it likely to interest the reader? Why?
- Does it start with a general statement related to the topic and gradually become more specific?
- Is there a thesis statement that tells the reader what the essay will be about? Can you easily identify it?
- Does the introduction give an overview of the essay structure?
- Are ideas clearly linked between sentences or is it sometimes confusing?
- Does it include a definition? Do you think a definition is necessary or would it be helpful?

5.4 Evaluate the introduction to a student's essay. Use the checklist in Task 5.3 as your criterion. Then complete the table of strengths and weaknesses.

<u>The advantages and disadvantages of genetically modified crops</u>

New developments in the field of genetically modified (GM) agriculture are reported almost daily as exciting new discoveries are made. These new developments have generally been welcomed by consumers. Recently, however, people have begun to realise how rapidly GM agriculture is spreading, so questions are being asked about its effects on our environment and health. Needless to say, farmers generally feel that high production levels and top-quality crops are more important than the possible negative side effects. In the light of such advantages, the influence of GM agriculture on the environment and on our health is, in my opinion, unimportant.

---

strengths	weaknesses

2

5.5 Choose one of the essay titles and write a possible introduction. Discuss the content and structure with a partner before you start writing.

> Food additives should be banned. Discuss.   Euthanasia should be made legal. Discuss.

> Outline the different types of alternative energy sources.

> What are the main benefits of investing money in space research?

> What would you do to improve the lives of the elderly in your country?

Essay writing: points to remember

- Planning and organisation are key skills.
- Keep a close eye on your title: always answer the question.
- Keep a note as you go along of all references or sources that you use.
- Redrafting is an essential skill.

Reflect

If you have an informed opinion about a subject, it can help you identify controlling ideas for a strong thesis statement.

Write down your opinion on the topics below. Then create thesis statements using your opinions as the controlling ideas.

a. Sugar is harmful to health and provides no benefits.

b. Animal conservation is a waste of time because extinction is part of the natural process of evolution.

3 The body of the essay

At the end of this unit, you will be able to:

- structure the main part of an academic essay
- plan and write effective paragraphs

If you want to write a successful academic essay, you need to have:
- an outline plan
- a clear structure
- a strong introduction
- logical and meaningful paragraphs
- a development of an argument or discussion
- a conclusion

The organisation of your essay will depend, to some extent, on what sort of essay you are writing. The body of your essay can be arranged in various logical ways, for example:
- reasons for and reasons against
- causes followed by effects
- problems followed by solutions

Task 1 Paragraph organisation

1.1 **Are the statements true (T) or false (F)? Discuss your answers as a class.**

a. Each main idea should be presented separately in a new paragraph. `T`

b. Each paragraph in the body of your essay will usually begin with a topic sentence stating the main idea of the paragraph.

c. The topic sentence should be followed by several sentences, which support the main idea.

d. To add support or evidence, you should use examples, figures or statistics.

e. You should always use quotations to support your ideas.

f. You should have a strong concluding sentence in each paragraph to link the reader back to the topic sentence or provide a link to the next paragraph or section.

1.2 Read the extract from a descriptive essay on the origins of Coca-Cola. Divide the text into five paragraphs.

The first episode in the Coca-Cola story is an important part of the rise of capitalism in the United States of America. Towards the end of the 19th century, America gradually began to transform itself from a nation of farmers to a city-based industrialised society. The industrial revolution was epitomised by new communications and the arrival and spread of the railways. This produced a new kind of capitalism, a distinctive American variety, where the ethos centred firmly on the image of individual immigrant struggle. The world of US business was on its way. One of the most important changes, which helped business success, was population growth. The American population almost doubled in size between 1880 and 1910, and a large proportion of the increase was created by the new immigrants from Europe and the rest of the world. Success came from ambition and hard work, and anybody could make large amounts of money provided they tried hard enough. Helped by the success of some, immigrants flocked to the USA. By 1890, there were already over 4,000 American millionaires and Andrew Carnegie, who had made a fortune from railways and iron and steel, was spreading the 'Gospel of Wealth'. There were, however, some disadvantages to the new business environment. In many parts of the USA, there was more than an element of the Wild West. Con men, thieves and swindlers came to the new towns that were appearing, looking for suitable victims. A second major disadvantage was that Coca-Cola was originally a patent medicine, and only about 2% of the medicines that were produced ever became well-known – most inventors and salesmen failed miserably. Thirdly, although large profits could be made from all kinds of medicines, many of which often cost almost nothing to produce, by the late 1880s, the market for medicines was already saturated. Patent medicines, therefore, were not an easy commercial area to break into. Another important aspect of the story is that the world of medicine was not advanced at this time. Nineteenth-century American doctors were not numerous, nor were they very good (anaesthetics were still to be invented and some of the primitive methods used by the medical profession were terrifying; killing more patients than they saved). This was the reason why many people turned to alternative remedies, the so-called patent medicines, to solve their health problems. By the end of the century, there were thousands of cures on offer for every imaginable ailment, from the common cold to malaria, all of which required extensive advertising in newspapers and public places to promote their superior values over their competitors. To conclude, it is not surprising that many would-be tycoons were attracted by the rising numbers of consumers and that the field of patent medicines was an attractive starting point for some. In 1869, Dr John Pemberton, a Georgia pharmacist, had moved to Atlanta searching to make his fortune by the discovery of the perfect patent cure. In 1886, after long years of research, he finally launched his new invention. It was into this very crowded and over-competitive market that Coca-Cola was to emerge as a highly successful product.

Task 2 Linking words and phrases

It is important to develop and link your ideas in each paragraph so the reader can follow your line of argument clearly. The Coca-Cola essay uses words and phrases to help the reader follow the sequence of events.

2.1 **Read the Coca-Cola essay on page 14 again. Match the words and phrases in the text that function in the same way as the linking words (a–e).**

a. Firstly   _The first episode_

b. Secondly   _____

c. Thirdly   _____

d. Fourthly   _____

e. Finally   _____

2.2 **Match the linking expressions in the box with their function (a–f).**

on the other hand	as shown by	due to	for instance
~~in the same way~~	as a result	equally important	since	like
despite	another important aspect	therefore	because of

a. showing similarity   _in the same way_

b. comparing or contrasting   _____

c. adding something   _____

d. giving reasons   _____

e. showing cause and effect   _____

f. giving an example   _____

3

Task 3 The topic sentence and supporting sentences

The *topic sentence* is usually at the beginning of a paragraph. When you write a paragraph, you should try to develop this initial idea and not change or add too many new ideas.

3.1 Consider the three possible topic sentences (a–c) for a paragraph on *The benefits of immigration to industrialised countries.* **Work with a partner to discuss which topic sentence is the most suitable. Circle the correct answer.**

   a.   Immigration is a very difficult subject to discuss because there are many possible different viewpoints.

   b.   One of the major problems of immigration is that people in the host country may disagree with such a policy.

   c.   Immigration can offer several clear advantages for industrialised countries.

3.2 **Read the two paragraphs. In each paragraph, the topic sentence has been underlined. Decide which paragraph develops the idea given in the topic sentence better. Discuss your reasons in groups.**

Paragraph A

There are obvious advantages to learning English in Britain. Every day there are opportunities to practise listening to and speaking with British people. In the first place, students can experience the culture first-hand, which is a great help when trying to understand the language. This is especially true if they choose to live with a British family as exchange students, for example. In addition, if students attend a language school full-time, the teachers will be native speakers. In this case, not only will students' speaking and listening skills improve, but attention can be given to developing reading and writing skills as well.

Paragraph B

Immigration to industrialised countries poses a number of difficult challenges for incoming families. They may need to learn a new language, they may face racism and discrimination and they frequently have problems adjusting to the new culture. In France, for example, it is illegal for Muslim schoolgirls to wear headscarves to school. Already, five Muslim schoolgirls have been expelled from school for wearing headscarves. The ban is perceived by many as intolerant, undermining the integration of France's Muslims. Feminists say the Islamic scarf is a repressive symbol, but many French Muslims say the ban is racist and against their human rights. 'Everyone has the right to freedom of thought, conscience and religion; this right includes freedom to manifest their religion or belief in teaching, practice, worship and observance' (Article 18, The Universal Declaration of Human Rights).

3.3 There are three thesis statements below. Write a topic sentence for statements 2 and 3. Then write a supporting sentence or two for the paragraph. Remember to focus on the main idea. The first has been done as an example.

Example

Thesis statement 1 *Young people who live at home while studying at university have several advantages.*

Paragraph 1

Topic sentence *First of all, they can focus on their studies without worrying about domestic matters.*

Supporting sentence(s) *Students living away from home have to learn how to do their own laundry and may well have to shop and cook for themselves. Those who live at home do not have such concerns.*

a. **Thesis statement 2** *The causes and effects of global warming will be briefly outlined in this essay.*

Paragraph 1

Topic sentence _____

_____

Supporting sentence(s) _____

_____

_____

_____

_____

b. **Thesis statement 3** *Personal computers have revolutionised communication and business practices in the past 20 years.*

Paragraph 1

Topic sentence _____

_____

Supporting sentence(s) _____

_____

_____

_____

_____

3

Task 4 Organising an essay

4.1 Below are the opening sentences of the paragraphs from the original Coca-Cola essay in Task 1. Identify the topic and put the paragraphs into the correct order.

paragraph begins	topic	order
Another important aspect of the story is that the world of medicine was not advanced at this time.		
There were, however, some disadvantages to the new business environment.		
To conclude, it is not surprising that many would-be tycoons were attracted by the rising numbers of consumers and that the field of patent medicines was an attractive starting point for some.		
One of the most important changes, which helped business success, was population growth.		
The first episode in the Coca-Cola story is an important part of the rise of capitalism in the United States of America.	the rise of capitalism	1

4.2 Work with a partner to answer the questions for each of the essay titles (1–5).

a. How would you structure your essay? e.g., *Reasons for and reasons against, causes followed by effects, problems followed by solutions*

b. What are the main points that you would include in the essay?

c. What sort of research will you have to do on this topic?

1. There is too much advertising on television. Discuss.

2. Discuss the advantages and disadvantages of English as a world language.

3. How has education improved over the last one hundred years?

4. Marketing is the most important aspect of a business's activities. Discuss.

5. Every individual has a responsibility to prevent global warming.

4.3 Choose one of the essay titles and make a plan for it. List the topics you would cover in each paragraph.

4.4 Practise writing the first paragraph of your essay. Make sure you start with a clear topic sentence.

Reflect

Look through examples of essays you or other students have written, with a view to developing your ability to recognise good essay organisation.

When you understand how to structure an essay, you will begin to notice whether other writers have been successful in doing this well or not. By sharpening your critical skills, you will find your own writing skills will automatically grow.

4 Effective conclusions

At the end of this unit, you will be able to:

• write a successful conclusion paragraph

The main aim of the *conclusion* is to show that you have successfully answered the question. It does not include any new information, but it summarises the main points made in the body of the essay. It should be clear and draw your argument to a close and, ideally, it needs to leave a strong impression on the reader.

Task 1 Restating the thesis

A strong conclusion should refer back to the thesis statement in your introduction.

1.1 **Read the thesis statement and conclusion of the same essay. Answer the questions.**

    a.   What is the subject of the essay? Think of a title for it.

    b.   How is the conclusion similar to and different from the introduction?

> **Thesis statement**
>
> The growth of a 'fast-food' culture in this country has generated unexpected problems, including rising obesity levels and, more importantly, the loss of our gastronomic heritage. This essay will examine the role of fast food in the development of an increasingly unhealthy Britain.

> **Conclusion**
>
> Fast-food outlets cannot entirely be blamed for our increasingly unhealthy dietary habits. Fast food evidently responds to a need in our modern society, and reflects changes in our modern lifestyle. It is, rather, our lifestyle which needs changing if we hope to become a healthier nation.

You need to repeat the main ideas in the conclusion, but you do not want to simply write the same sentences again. One way of linking back to the thesis statement is to rewrite it (that is, to paraphrase the ideas and the language). You can use synonyms, rearrange the order and also change some of the grammar to do this.

1.2 **Returning to your essay on the problems associated with traffic congestion, look at the extract from an introduction below. Think of synonyms for the underlined words and write them in the table.**

> Lack of investment in public transport is having serious consequences for travellers in Britain today; this is the major point that will be discussed in this essay.

original	synonym
lack of	
consequences	
travellers	
major point	
discussed	

1.3 **Rewrite the sentence, using synonyms and a different word order to make a good concluding statement. Think about the grammar that needs to change (e.g., *will be* is not appropriate for a conclusion).**

Task 2 Organising the concluding paragraph

2.1 **Put the sentences in order (1–5) to form an effective conclusion for an essay on the problems of urban overcrowding.**

a. ____ Government policies aimed at solving these problems are too often very simple measures that offer only short-term solutions.

b. _I_ In conclusion, urban overcrowding causes problems on all levels.

c. ____ It is a model which aims for improved social conditions and offers a high quality of life for city dwellers, whatever their number.

d. ____ This essay has argued for the implementation of a long-term policy which needs to provide an economically sustainable, resource efficient model of city design.

e. ____ The creation of such a model will help to resolve many of the current and future problems of urban life.

2.2 **Evaluate the effectiveness of this concluding paragraph. Identify …**

a. a restatement of the argument or thesis. ☐

b. a summary of the main points covered in the essay. ☐

c. a reasoned and logical evaluation of your argument. ☐

d. a comment on future implications or a recommendation. ☐

4

Task 3 Finishing with a clear statement

3.1 Look back at the thesis statement you wrote in Unit 2, Task 4.3, in which you stated the focus of your essay. Draw your argument to a close with a concluding sentence which refers back to your introduction. Try to use synonyms, paraphrases and different grammatical structures.

3.2 Sometimes it may be useful to draft a rough conclusion first, so that you know what you will say at the end of the essay. Can you think of any advantages or disadvantages of this approach? Discuss them and write them in the table.

advantages	disadvantages

Task 4 Lecturer expectations

4.1 Tutors and lecturers have clear ideas of what they want to see in the conclusion of an academic essay. Read and check that you understand the expectations. Identify whether you think you are strong or weak in these areas.

expectations	I am good/OK/weak at …
clear links between the introduction and conclusion	
a concluding paragraph that leaves a strong impression on the reader	
a restatement of the main points in your essay	
a logical conclusion to the argument outlined in the essay	
a comment on implications or a recommendation for the future	
an answer to the question set (task completion)	

Reflect

Look at an essay you or another student has written and think about how you can improve the conclusion to reflect the content of the essay. Think about how this process helps you focus on what the essay is saying.

Reflect on how the effort put into a conclusion will help you think more carefully about the assignment as a whole.

5 Academic style and register

At the end of this unit, you will be able to:

* identify some of the features of academic style
* use formal, objective language
* use cautious language (hedging) to avoid making false claims

Task 1 Formal or informal register?

Academic essays usually require a formal style. You need to remember what to avoid in an academic essay.

1.1 **Compare the two definitions of *geography*. Write the features of formal/written, academic style in the table on the opposite page. Discuss your findings with a partner.**

Informal/spoken:

> Geography? Well, I think it's basically just some sort of mix of physical and social sciences and how they interact together. You know, like, for example, how global warming has an effect on the economy, um, of a region …, but you can also look at these things individually too … er … so you could just study things like sea-level rise, which'd be physical, or you could look at … say … how people, human beings, adapt themselves to the environment, that's human.

Formal/written:

> Geography is the study of the surface of the Earth, the location and distribution of its physical and cultural features, and the interrelation of these features as they affect humans. In the study of geography, two main branches may be distinguished, physical geography and human geography.

1.2 **What other features of formal discourse are in the definitions? Add these features to the table.**

1.3 **Read the sentences (a–l) and decide if they are formal (F) or informal (I). Explain your answers, and add any further examples to the table.**

a.	I don't believe this is true at all. It sounds like nonsense.	I
b.	New regulations will come into effect next year.	
c.	The study was conducted with a group of school-age children.	
d.	We're definitely going to have to follow those stupid new rules next year.	
e.	Further analysis is required before conclusions can be drawn.	
f.	It really puzzles me why some students don't get better grades.	
g.	Our experiments were OK – they just proved that his argument didn't stand up.	
h.	He'll have to have a better look at the findings before making his mind up.	
i.	It has been proved that the claims are unfounded.	
j.	We went down to a school and chatted with some of the kids.	
k.	It isn't clear why quite a lot of students don't get really good grades.	
l.	A major aspect of the investigation involved research into social housing trends.	

feature	formal/written examples
use of contractions: *isn't*, *don't*, etc.	
use of fillers: *well*, *er*, etc.	
use of passive voice	
impersonal and objective	
personal and subjective	
punctuation	

Task 2 Cautious language

Another typical feature of academic writing is the need to be careful or cautious. Unless you are quoting a fact or a statistic, or there is evidence which shows 100% certainty, statements and conclusions are often qualified in some way to make them less assertive or positive. The reason is partly English academic style, but it is also to avoid making any false claims. This use of cautious language is sometimes called *hedging*.

2.1 **Read the statements. How certain is the writer of the truth of each claim? Which words indicate the level of certainty?**

   a.   The new vaccine might prevent the spread of Ebola.

   b.   The new vaccine will probably prevent the spread of Ebola.

   c.   The new vaccine will prevent the spread of Ebola.

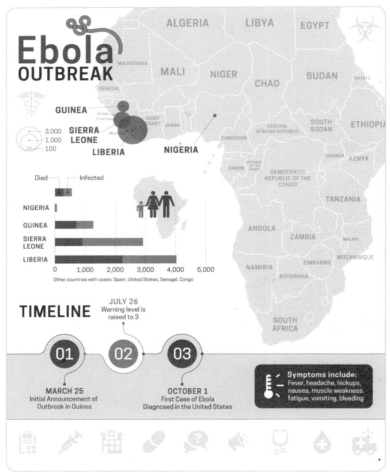

2.2 **Compare the statements. Which statement is presented as a fact? Identify the hedging words or expressions used to make the other statements less assertive. Which phrase distances the writer from the claim?**

   a.   Drinking green tea appears to lower the risk of developing cancer.

   b.   Drinking green tea lowers the risk of developing cancer.

   c.   Some studies suggest that drinking green tea can lower the risk of developing certain cancers.

The sentences you write will depend on the strength of the evidence available to you at the time of writing and how certain you are that the evidence is true.

2.3 **Read the eight sentence pairs. Work in pairs to discuss what sort of language is used in the second sentence of each pair to make it less assertive or positive.**

a.　1.　Some colleges and universities in this country have large numbers of international students.

　　2.　Some colleges and universities in this country <u>appear to have</u> large numbers of international students.

b.　1.　Instead of coming here, international students should study in their own country.

　　2.　It could be argued that, instead of coming here, international students should study in their own country.

c.　1.　This is a misapplication of government policy.

　　2.　This would seem to be a misapplication of government policy.

d.　1.　This is true.

　　2.　To a certain extent, this may be true.

e.　1.　Erlichman's findings prove that the amount of independent study is directly related to higher performance levels.

　　2.　Erlichman's findings suggest that the amount of independent study might be directly related to higher performance levels.

f.　1.　Inflation will not rise next year.

　　2.　Evidence indicates that inflation will probably not rise next year.

g.　1.　The survey demonstrates that English schoolchildren do not want to learn more foreign languages.

　　2.　The survey tends to indicate that English schoolchildren are apparently not in favour of learning more foreign languages.

h.　1.　There are situations where this is the only solution.

　　2.　There are undoubtedly situations where this would seem to be the only possible solution.

2.4 **Underline the hedging expressions used in the second sentence of each pair above and then write the example in the appropriate place in the table.**

hedging feature	example
hedging verbs	... appear to have ...
use of modal verbs	
qualifying expressions	
probability adjectives and adverbs	
frequency adverbs	

5

Task 3 Register in use

Informal English uses everyday spoken forms (colloquialisms) that are inappropriate for formal written English. It is important not to mix styles in academic writing.

3.1 Below is a paragraph from the Coca-Cola essay you looked at in Unit 3, Task 1.2, rewritten in a much more informal style.

Underline the parts that are too colloquial. Look particularly carefully at the vocabulary and the sentence structure.

> A massive change – one which really helped business – was more people arriving in the USA. There were two times as many people who got here between 1880 and 1910, and lots of them came from all sorts of different places, like Europe. If you wanted to be successful you had to work really hard; however, you could get rich quickly if you did this. Lots of immigrants made it and because of this, lots more wannabe millionaires turned up in the US. By 1890, America maybe had around 4,000 millionaires. One of the best was Andrew Carnegie, who got rich through trains and iron and steel. His message was called the 'Gospel of Wealth'.

3.2 Go back and check your answers with the original paragraph in Unit 3, Task 1.2.

3.3 The following extract from an essay is written in a mixed style with colloquialisms and other inappropriate words. Rewrite it in a more academic style using:
- appropriate vocabulary and grammatical structures
- cautious language (Unit 5, Task 2)

> Another kind of useful alternative fuel is electricity. This isn't really a very efficient fuel right now, because the technology is somewhat limited; however, it's fair to say that recent advances in the production of electric cars could maybe make this a reality in the future. But it is possible for cars powered with electricity to release little or no emissions, so if we want this alternative fuel to become a reality, we'll need it in lots of cars. Maybe then it'll make some sort of a difference. If we want this to happen, i.e., to knock a big chunk out of the pollution problem all around the world, it'll take a while.

Reflect

Read through an essay that you have recently written, looking carefully at the language you used. Bearing in mind what you have learned about the appropriate level of formality, do you feel that you could improve the way you express yourself?

Also, check that the tone of the essay is not too assertive and explore whether it would benefit from more hedging expressions.

Guidelines for the future

At the end of this unit, you will be able to:

- understand the editing and redrafting processes in essay writing
- understand what lecturers expect from a piece of academic writing

Task 1 Things to remember

1.1 **You should now be familiar with some of the main principles of essay writing. Check the following and decide which areas you will need to work on in the future.**

- understanding the task
- checking the title carefully
- answering the question set
- getting organised
- keeping to deadlines
- writing a plan
- collecting and recording sources and important information
- keeping useful phrases and examples of 'essay language'
- reflecting on what you have written
- checking and redrafting language and content
- writing a final draft
- presenting your essay in a clear and acceptable form

Task 2 Redrafting

2.1 **Correct and rewrite the draft based on the feedback given by the tutor.**

> source?   Sp.   gr.   tense
> It was <u>forcast</u> that the number of robbery would <u>have risen</u> by 29% in (l)ondon between (a)pril
>   wrong word   tense
> 2001 and (m)arch 2002 but the <u>real</u> ? figures show that the overall number of crimes <u>was falling</u>
>   watch punctuation

6

2.2 **Answer the questions.**

    a.   How many drafts of an essay should you write?

    b.   What do you need to consider and work on when you redraft an essay?

2.3 **Make a list of the answers to Task 2.2, question b. Some examples are given below to help you.**

redrafting: things to work on	considerations
paragraphs	• the right structure • each paragraph has a main idea • paragraphs are in the right order
grammar	
length of essay	

Task 3 How to get a better mark

Remember that your mark will depend not only on how good your writing is, but also on how successfully you have completed the task. It is important to make sure you read and understand the feedback that your lecturer gives you to help you with your next essay. It is also important to understand the marking criteria.

For instance, robbery might be decreased whereas murder has increased so the total number of
good to include e.g.   *Sp.*
crimes has decreased. This is because the <u>goverment</u> always show their performance in a positive

way. *ref? – this is rather a generalisation!*

3.1 **Read some comments that lecturers sometimes make about students' writing.**
Which comments indicate that the lecturer thinks you have done what was required?

   a.   You have written a competent answer, but, unfortunately, it is an answer to a different question!

   b.   Your essay would be improved by checking the grammar and spelling.

   c.   You have answered the question very well; you show a good understanding of the issues and have provided some excellent examples.

   d.   There is little evidence in the essay of reflective and evaluative thought. Your conclusion is rather weak.

   e.   The essay needs to be word-processed – in general, the presentation is very poor.

   f.   You have made good use of personal reflection and have clearly done a lot of background reading on the topic.

   g.   You have described the situation well, but you have not analysed the advantages and disadvantages as the question asked you to do.

3.2 **Can you add any other comments that teachers have made about <u>your</u> writing?**

3.3 Study the marking criteria below for essay writing and match them with the appropriate percentage bands below. *Note: 40% is the pass mark in this scheme.*

| 70%+ |
| 60–69% |
| 50–59% |
| 40–49% |
| 30–39% |

marking criteria	mark
ideas generally not made clear and often irrelevant; weak paragraphs; small range of vocabulary; grammatical structure is very limited	
ideas generally clear, but not always very relevant; some lack of paragraphing; limited range of vocabulary; limited grammatical structure at times	
lacks any satisfactory organisation or development of ideas; vocabulary use very weak; unsatisfactory use of grammatical structure; generally fails to meet the required pass standard	
excellent text organisation; clear paragraphs with well-expressed ideas; wide range of vocabulary; good use of grammatical structure	
good text organisation with generally relevant ideas; adequate range of vocabulary and grammatical structure	

Task 4 A model essay

4.1 Read the essay title and underline the instruction verbs.

> Discuss the problems associated with urban overcrowding and evaluate possible solutions.

4.2 Read the introduction to the essay and answer the questions.

    a.   How does the writer arouse your interest?

    b.   What is the thesis statement?

Introduction

The 20th century saw a major increase in the world's population and, at the same time, the emergence of a global society driven by the forces of economics and industry. People were inexorably drawn towards living in towns and cities, migrating from rural communities out of economic necessity. As a result of this influx, modern-day cities across the globe face serious problems due to overcrowding. The most critical include poverty and homelessness, unemployment, the provision of adequate health care and education, and knock-on effects such as rising crime and pollution. This essay will identify solutions to some of these problems of urban overcrowding and evaluate their feasibility.

4.3 Read the main body of the essay on the opposite page and answer the questions. Remember the introduction verbs in the essay title and the thesis statement, while you read.

a. Underline the topic sentence in each paragraph in the essay and make a note of its key words.

b. How much support does the writer give for the topic sentence in each paragraph? Make a note (key words only) of the support below.

Paragraph 1

Topic sentence key words: <u>Urban overcrowding = has become a global phenomenon</u>

Support (examples and evidence):   _____

Paragraph 2

Topic sentence key words: _____

Support (examples and evidence):   _____

Paragraph 3

Topic sentence key words: _____

Support (examples and evidence):   _____

Paragraph 4

Topic sentence key words: _____

Support (examples and evidence):   _____

Paragraph 5

Topic sentence key words: _____

Support (examples and evidence):   _____

4.4 Compare your answers to Task 4.3 with a partner's. Decide which paragraph(s):

a. describe the situation and causes   _____

b. suggest solutions   _____

c. describe the problems   _____

Main body

Urban overcrowding is not a recent phenomenon, but it has recently become a global demographic problem. The rise of the world's 'megacities', such as Tokyo, Jakarta, São Paulo and Cairo, with populations approaching 20 million, is one of the most marked trends of recent decades. In 1950, for example, New York City was unique among the world's cities in having more than 10 million inhabitants. By 1975, that number had grown to 15 million. By 2015, it is estimated it will reach 21 million (UNO, 2005). Two principal reasons for this phenomenon can be identified, one economic and the other sociocultural.

People migrate to cities in search of both economic security and improved social conditions. As the economy of a nation develops, its cities develop as centres of industry, investment and education, providing plentiful job opportunities for those in search of a higher standard of living. Sydney, São Paulo and Frankfurt are all thriving modern cities, which have developed exponentially since the Second World War. A further example is Tokyo, the hub for Japan's rapid economic development in the 1960s and 70s; its population grew quickly as people moved there to find employment, and it is now the most populous city in the world (population 35.3 million).

Not all developing nations, however, are equipped to cope with such rapidly expanding city populations. The overriding problem associated with overcrowding is poverty and its attendant social deprivations – homelessness, unemployment and insecurity. Immigrants to cities from rural areas are typically the poorest members of urban society and, in many cities, are often forced to live in shanty towns or slums on the periphery of the city without access to clean drinking water or safe sanitation, in cramped and unsanitary conditions. Examples of such poor living conditions can be seen across the continents, from Caracas to Bombay. Unemployment is widespread as families fight to survive. Transmission of infectious diseases is very common in such conditions, resulting too frequently in high infant mortality rates (UNESCO, 2002). Furthermore, access to vital social services, such as hospitals and schools, may be restricted as authorities try to cope with large numbers of people, thus denying children adequate education and health care.

Inevitably, there is no one best solution to a problem of such magnitude. Two solutions are proposed, both of which seek to move people away from the cities. The first is that of resettlement, where government-led housing initiatives seek to rehouse families on the outskirts of cities. The Shanghai Housing Settlement Project, begun in 1987, is an example of successful urban renewal, where living conditions have been measurably improved. Resolution of the housing shortage has promoted long-term social development and stability, resulting in social and economic benefits. This measure does not, however, address the problem of urban sprawl as the city spreads outwards, but it does relieve the pressure of urban overcrowding.

The second solution encourages the relocation of businesses, factories and warehouses to rural areas. It exploits brownfield sites in the countryside, which are developed as business parks. Policies of industrial relocation have been successful in Canada and the UK, where industrial expansion of cities has been curtailed. However, people are not willing to leave the cities unless they are guaranteed better housing, schools and transport facilities, so long-term government investment in these areas is crucial. Furthermore, such projects are disputed by environmentalists, who see the developments as a threat to the balance of the countryside.

4.5 Read the conclusion to the essay and answer the questions. (While you read, remember the important verbs in the essay title and the thesis statement in the introduction.)

a. Is there any new information in the conclusion?

b. How does the conclusion link back to the introduction?

Conclusion

In conclusion, urban overcrowding causes problems on all levels. Government policies aimed at solving these problems are too often simple stopgap measures offering only short-term solutions. This essay has argued for the implementation of a long-term policy that potentially provides an economically sustainable, resource-efficient model of city design. It is a model that fulfils a universal desire for improved social conditions and, ultimately, offers a high quality of life for city dwellers, whatever their number.

4.6 Read the whole essay again. Decide where you could make changes from assertive to more cautious hedging language. Complete the table with your changes.

change from	to

Task 5 The problem–solution essay

The model essay in Task 4 is an example of the problem–solution model. The pattern of organisation commonly used in writing when analysing a problem is:

Situation		Problem		Solution		Evaluation
A situation is given.	→	The problem of the situation is identified.	→	A solution to the problem is presented.	→	An evaluation is given.

5.1 **Read the text. Underline the parts of the text that:**
- describe the situation
- identify the problem
- suggest a solution(s)
- evaluate the solution(s)

Recent evidence confirms that global warming is melting the ice in Antarctica faster than had been previously thought. Scientists say the rise in sea levels around the world caused by the melting may have been underestimated. It is thought that over 13,000 km^2 of sea ice in the Antarctic Peninsula have been lost over the last 50 years. This poses a major problem because its effects will be felt across the globe.

A rise in sea levels increases the level of wave attack and tides, causing changes in the stability of shorelines, as well as flooding of lowlands. In many places, a 50-cm rise would see entire beaches being washed away by erosion, together with a significant chunk of the coastline. Many island nations will have their supplies of drinking water reduced because sea water will invade their freshwater aquifers. While some islands have sizeable populations, they are insignificant compared with the tens of millions of people living in the low-level coastal areas of Southern Asia. These include the coastlines of Pakistan, India, Sri Lanka, Bangladesh and Burma.

Since more than 75% of the human population live within 60 km of a coast, finding a solution is imperative. While implementation of flood prevention measures on a local level is helpful in the short term, there is no physical capacity that humans have to protect against long-term sea-level rise. The key to coping with the rise in sea levels is education about the effects and accurate assessments of hazards for given points in time. In this way, humans can act decisively and appropriately to minimise loss of life and economic and ecological impacts. Education is the only long-term, far-reaching solution to sea-level rise.

5.2 Complete the flow chart with notes based on the text you read in Task 5.1.

Situation

⬇

Problem

⬇

Solution

⬇

Evaluation

Task 6 Write an essay outline

6.1 Prepare an essay outline for the following essay question (or one of the other questions in this module). Follow the steps.

> English has become a global language because it is both easy to learn and superior to other languages. Discuss.

- Analyse the question: How many general statements are there? What is the main instruction verb?
- Brainstorm ideas using one of the techniques from Unit 1, Task 3.
- Write a thesis statement to show how your argument will develop through the essay.
- Decide which essay pattern to use (Unit 3).
- Link your ideas into a logical sequence and decide how many paragraphs you will use.
- Write a topic sentence for each paragraph.
- Note the supporting evidence and examples for each of your main points.
- Refer to the *Referencing & Avoiding Plagiarism* module in the TASK series, if you are including quotations.

6.2 Work in groups to discuss your essay outlines.

Reflect

You should now feel more confident about what is required in writing a formal academic essay. Write a list of six new ideas for better academic writing that you have learned from this module and that you did not know before.

Use the list as a checklist when you next write an essay for your studies and you should find you obtain a better grade.

Web work

Website 1

Andy Gillett's Using English for Academic Purposes

http://www.uefap.com/writing/writfram.htm

Review

This is a very useful study skills site written by Andy Gillett at the University of Hertfordshire.

Task

Click on the 'Exercises' link on the panel and complete each exercise. Begin with 'Questions: Understanding the Question' and apply your knowledge from this module.

Website 2

University of New England Academic Writing Learning hub

http://learninghub.une.edu.au/tlc/aso/aso-online/academic-writing/sample-essay.php

Review

This is a useful interactive site from the University of New England in Australia.

Task

This link takes you to a sample academic essay. Complete the exercise entitled 'Analyse an Academic Essay'.

Extension activities

Activity 1

Prepare an essay outline for the essay question. Use the same steps as you did in Unit 6, Task 6.

> Discuss the problems associated with urbanisation in your country and evaluate possible solutions.

Activity 2

Write an essay.

Expand one of your essay outlines into a full essay. Although you may have a number of essays to write over the year, it is useful to write one immediately on completing this module.

You can complete one that you have been working on in this module, or choose an area to write about that you are particularly interested in.

Glossary

academic writing (n) Writing that students and academics produce. It normally involves research, demonstrates learning or knowledge and follows clear conventions in its style and organisation. For example, essays, assignments, reports, dissertations and theses.

analyse (v) To break an issue down into parts in order to study, identify and discuss their meaning and/or relevance.

analytical essay (n) An essay that involves analysing a text, theory or set of ideas.

argument essay (n) An essay that involves building a case for an idea or thesis statement. This entails giving reasons for your thesis statement and providing evidence to back it up.

brainstorm (v) The act of writing down all the thoughts and ideas you have about a topic without stopping to monitor, edit or organise them. Brainstorming is a creative process that can be done alone or in a group.

colloquial (adj) Used to describe informal spoken words and expressions used in conversation, or informal written language used in letters to friends and family or emails. For example, in British English, a colloquial way of saying 'Don't be annoyed!' would be 'Chill out!'

deadline (n) The date or time by which an assignment or project needs to be completed.

descriptive essay (n) An essay that describes a process or sequence of events rather than arguing, interpreting or evaluating.

draft (n) (v) 1 (n) An early version of a piece of academic writing that is used as the starting point for further work. 2 (v) To create an early version of an essay, knowing that you will go back afterwards and develop and edit your language and ideas.

edit (v) To select, rearrange and improve material to make it more suitable for its final purpose. Editing material involves reorganising it, correcting errors, improving the wording or content and changing its length, by adding sections or taking them out.

evaluate (v) To assess information in terms of quality, relevance, objectivity and accuracy.

evaluative essay (n) An essay that requires you to either compare and evaluate a range of things in relation to one another, or to look at the arguments for and against one thing, and come to a judgement in your conclusion. It is asking for your personal opinion, backed up with facts, examples and explanations.

exemplify (v) To illustrate a belief, statement or theory with examples. You may be asked to do this in an essay.

free writing (v) To write without deliberate or conscious thought so that ideas flow freely. This is sometimes done as an exercise to stimulate ideas and creativity in preparation for a written assignment.

hedging (n) The use of deliberately vague, uncertain language in order to avoid asserting something as a fact that may not be true. In the context of academic writing, hedging language is often used to discuss theories and possible solutions.

key skill (n) A skill that is important to master in order to be successful in a certain area, such as academic life or employment.

marking criteria (n) A list of criteria or qualities that the person who marks an assignment or exam is looking for, including aspects of the style, presentation and organisation of the work. For example, one criterion for an assignment that is graded above 70% (a first) is likely to be that it must include original ideas.

mind map (n) A diagram used to represent words, ideas, tasks or other items linked to, and arranged radially around, a central key word or idea.

objective (adj) (n) 1 (adj) An opinion or idea that is not influenced by personal feelings or emotions. 2 (n) The aim or what you want to achieve from an activity.

outline (n) A brief plan that shows the order in which you will deal with the main issues or ideas in a piece of academic writing.

paraphrase (v) To alter a piece of text so that you restate it (concisely) in different words without changing its meaning. It is useful to paraphrase when writing a summary of someone's ideas; if the source is acknowledged, it is not plagiarism. It is also possible to paraphrase your own ideas in an essay or presentation; that is, to state them again, often in a clearer, expanded way.

proofread (v) To read through a piece of writing and pick out and correct errors in it. It is useful to ask someone else to proofread your work. This should be done before the final draft of a piece of academic writing is submitted.

redraft (v) To write out a new draft of an essay, incorporating changes and making additions. This is done after you have read through, edited and/or had feedback on the first draft.

reference (n) (v) 1 (n) Acknowledgement of the sources of ideas and information that you use in written work and oral presentations. 2 (v) To acknowledge or mention the sources of information.

register (n) The style of speech or writing that is used in a specific context and/or by a specific group of people. For example, a student will use a very informal, colloquial register to text or email a friend, but a formal scientific register to write a Chemistry report.

restate (v) To paraphrase or say something again in a different way. This is often done in essays to help clarify an idea or issue. The conclusion of an essay will often restate the original thesis statement in more depth.

source (n) Something (usually a book, article or other text) that supplies you with information. In an academic context, sources used in essays and reports must be acknowledged.

structure (n) (v) 1 (n) A framework or arrangement of several parts, put together in a particular way. 2 (v) In academic writing, to put together ideas, arguments or thoughts in an organised, logical way. It is important to structure essays and presentations as you work on them.

subjective (adj) Describes an idea or opinion that is based on someone's personal opinions, rather than on observable phenomena.

supporting evidence (n) Information from academic sources that should be included in a piece of academic writing. This evidence illustrates and backs up your ideas and adds 'academic weight' to your work.

supporting sentences (n) Sentences that usually follow and systematically develop the idea contained in the topic sentence.

synonym (n) A word or phrase which has a similar meaning to another one and can replace it in a sentence without changing the meaning of the sentence.

technique (n) A method or way of doing something. For example, it is possible to learn useful techniques for answering exam questions.

thesis statement (n) A statement that explains the controlling idea or main argument (thesis) in a piece of academic writing. It is stated in the introduction and supported by reasons in the main body of the essay.

topic sentence (n) A sentence that states and sometimes summarises the topic/main idea of the paragraph and the standpoint taken by the writer. It usually comes at the beginning of each paragraph.

Notes

Notes

Notes

Notes

Published by
Garnet Publishing Ltd.
8 Southern Court
South Street
Reading RG1 4QS, UK

ISBN 978 1 78260 179 1

British Library Cataloguing-in-Publication Data
A catalogue record for this book is available from the British Library.

Production
Project manager: Clare Chandler
Editorial team: Clare Chandler, Kate Kemp
Design & Layout: Madeleine Maddock
Photography: iStockphoto

Garnet Publishing and the authors of TASK would like to thank the staff and students of the International Foundation Programme at the University of Reading for their respective roles in the development of these teaching materials.

Garnet Publishing would like to thank Paul Harvey for his contribution to the First edition of the TASK series.

All website URLs provided in this publication were correct at the time of printing. If any URL does not work, please contact your tutor, who will help you find similar resources.

Printed and bound in Lebanon by International Press: interpress@int-press.com

Acknowledgements

Page 16: Task 3.2, Paragraph A, *202 Useful Exercises for IELTS* by Garry Adams and Terry Peck, reproduced with kind permission of Adams & Austen Press.